August 10th
2011

My dear Barbara,

Enjoy — when you
pass it on for it's meant
to see a need for your own —
greater than your own —
Always with
love for you

Aunt Joan

Nature is my mentor, her muses guide me well... this book is my humble offering. Many special people have also inspired me: Susan Racinet, Kris McCormack, Kevin Droski (again & always) and my dear Mother... thank you all for your insight & encouragement.

Walk In Beauty

Written & Illustrated by

Lynne Gerard

the C.R. Gibson Company
Norwalk, Connecticut 06856

I would like to
share some thoughts
with you...
to encourage
you, to inspire you
and to remind you
how wonderful
you really are.

Try to remember
you are touched by, and
dwell in, all nuances of
goodness and
beauty ...

And yet, just as it is for everyone, there are times you may feel out of balance, out of touch -- disconnected.

A personal loss,
an unexpected change,
even the routine of day to
day tasks and responsibilities
can sometimes seem
overwhelming... and
separate you from the
rhythm of
life.

There are also
times when you
may feel blue
for no apparent
reason --
you reach to the
sky and feel
nothing...
no hope,
no joy,
no answer.

In my
own life, in
times such as
these, I often
discover I have
overlooked the
value of simple
pleasures.
Perhaps it
is the same for
you, too?

I do believe
life contains infinite
possibilities,
as innumerable as
the array of stars
in the night sky.
My life,
and your life, have
special glittering
places in this
world, reflecting
unlimited
potential.

We are
wonderfully linked
to the past and
brightly bound to
the future.
Here-and-now
is vastly rich in
heritage and fresh
with new
opportunities.

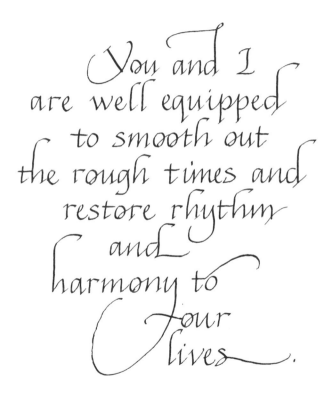

You and I
are well equipped
to smooth out
the rough times and
restore rhythm
and
harmony to
our
lives.

When you feel
as if dark clouds are
pressing down,
it is helpful to
redirect your focus
and take time for
reflection and
creative
expression.

Expressions of
your own
creativity are
vital to your
spirit... they assist
you in dealing
with difficulties
when
they arise.

Take a break,
make a pause-- let
the rest of the world
go by...

...for a moment or two stop planning, stop organizing and stop speeding away time. Abandon haste and worry. Walk in beauty.

Walk in beauty.
Surround yourself
with that which
pleases your
senses;
be it
delicately
fragrant
flowers,

compelling music,
or simply an evocative
thought.
         By nourishing
      your spirit
you gain the
      power to uplift
         your
      perceptions.

Walk in
beauty, and you
reunite yourself
with
the mystery of the
heavens
and the marvels
of nature.

Walk in
beauty, and you
develop the
capacity to perceive
and understand
the abiding goodness
woven into the
pattern of
time.

Just as
a caterpillar
is transformed
into a butterfly,
you
will
be reborn.

Just as the winter wind gives way to gentle breezes and budding flowers, you will adopt a fresh, youthful exuberance for all things.

See how a
tiny seed
hidden in the
ground becomes
a strong, saged
tree... let this
evidence of
potential fulfilled
strengthen
you.

Express yourself.
Write a poem,
or perhaps sing a song,
dance a dance,
paint a picture —
free your imagination...

... rearrange your furniture, cook a tasty meal, prune the hedges and weed your garden ~ do it with creative flair.

Such simple acts,
creatively expressed, are
so effective in making
dark days seem
brighter.   Thought-filled
actions give you a
sense of belonging and
connection... they can
bring you joy and
renew your hope.

No matter
what the
future
holds,
no matter
how harsh
the
wind
blows...

...when we
walk in beauty
we find the
inspiration
and strength
to
embrace today
and
welcome
tomorrow.